# Corresponding with a German Penfriend

These materials have emerged from the work done in Lothian
Region's Project on Graded Levels of Achievement in Foreign
Language Learning (GLAFLL)

*Compiled by*

## Judith Hamilton

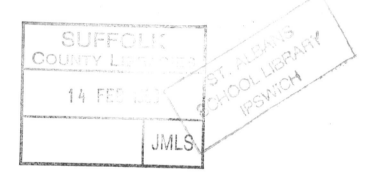

## Macmillan Education
London and Basingstoke

GERMAN LANGUAGE
LETTERS

# FOREWORD

This material has developed out of Lothian Region's project on Graded Levels of Achievement in Foreign Language Learning (GLAFLL). The material should be related to the *Syllabus Guidelines for a Graded Communicative Approach towards School Foreign Language Learning* by John Clark and Judith Hamilton published by the Centre for Information on Language Teaching and Research, 20 Carlton House Terrace, London, SW1Y 5AP, where the rationale and framework for GLAFLL have been set out. The material is related to B2 in Part 1 Communication of the Syllabus Guidelines.

The material is intended as practice material for penfriend exchanges. It can be used in S1—S4 (Scotland) or years 1—5 (England). It is intended for GLAFLL Stages 1 and 2, and there are separate sets of questions for each Stage. Some letters may well be appropriate as stimulus letters for Stages 3 to 5. Some teachers may find the material useful for CSE and other examination work.

The letters included are genuine letters which have been received by pupils in Lothian from their German penfriends, though some of the more glaring errors have been corrected as considered appropriate by Foreign Assistants.

Purposeful tasks have been set based on the letters. At Stage 1 pupils are expected to be able to understand the letters and to reply in English. They may be asked to explain the letter received to a third party in English. By Stage 2 pupils are expected to reply bilingually or entirely in German after they have checked their comprehension of the letter received. It is likely that the replies in German will contain a number of errors. It is suggested that teachers deal first with those errors which interfere with a clear understanding of meaning, building up to a gradual systematic treatment of repeated serious errors according to the aspirations and level of the individual pupil.

Answers have been provided for the questions so that the material can be used by pupils independently from the teacher as appropriate, and the material is preceded by a list of contents stating the topics in the letters and tasks for the pupils. One way of using the material would be for pupils to select the letters that most interest them, at whichever Stage they feel confident, and work through them at their own speed. A specimen pupil profile form is included to demonstrate one way of recording such work.

Some extra letters have been included at the end for the benefit of teachers who may wish to use them in their own way.

## *Contributors*

Many Lothian teachers, particularly those involved in the GLAFLL German Group, and a number of Foreign Assistants have contributed to the production of these materials.

Helen Laing, Dorothy Mullen and Tom McEwan produced the illustrations.

First published 1984
Reprinted 1985, 1987

Published by
MACMILLAN EDUCATION LTD
Houndmills, Basingstoke, Hampshire RG21 2XS
and London
Companies and representatives
throughout the world

Printed in Great Britain by
Tisbury Printing Ltd
Salisbury

*British Library Cataloguing in Publication Data*

Hamilton, Judith
   Corresponding with a German penfriend.
   —(Graded levels of achievement in foreign
   language learning/Lothian Region
   Council)
   1. German language—Grammar—
   1950—
   I. Title    II. Series
   438.2'421    PF3112

   ISBN 0—333—36617—4

# CONTENTS

## LETTER 1

*STAGE 1*

You are Shelley. Your class recently sent a request to a German school for penfriends. Opposite is a letter from a German pupil who wants to be your penfriend. Your friends have also had letters and want to know who you are going to write to. Here are some of the questions you are asked:

| 1 | Is your letter from a boy or a girl? | (1) |
|---|---|---|
| 2 | What is the name of your penfriend? | (1) |
| 3 | How old is your penfriend? | (1) |
| 4 | What does your penfriend look like? | (2) |
| 5 | What hobbies does he/she have? | (3) |
| 6 | What singers does he/she like? | (2) |

Check your answers with the Answer section, giving yourself the marks indicated above. Seven out of ten or more is very good indeed: try the Stage 2 task next.

*STAGE 2*

You are Shelley. This is your first letter from your new German penfriend, Anja. Write back to Anja, in German as much as possible, telling Anja about yourself as she has done in her letter.

Check the answers to see if you have picked up all the points in the letter.

4

Ich bin ein
Mädchen.

Liebe Shelley!

Ich heiße Anja Augenstein
bin auch wie du 12
Jahre alt. Ich habe
Dunkelblondes Haar und
blaue Augen.
Meine Hobbys sind:
Tanzen, Popmusik hören,
Englisch lesen, und Englisch
übersetzen, außerdem Fahre ich
gerne Rad.
Ich bin Fan für:
Blondie, Jazoo, Ideal
Ich gehe in die 7 Klasse!
Meine Adresse ist:
Anja Augenstein
47 Hamm 4
Kleinweg 5

## LETTER 2

*STAGE 1*

Your friend Janice has got her first penfriend letter from Daniela in Berlin. It is quite long and Janice will need some help with it. Explain the easy bits first:

1   What is the weather like in Berlin just now?                                                   (1)

2   Look at the bit which starts 'Mein Steckbrief'. It tells lots of things about Daniela. Check them off by first copying out and then filling in the form below:

| | |
|---|---|
| *Name:*  Daniela Dunst | *Age:* |
| *Birthday:* | *Height:* |
| *Colour of hair:* | *Colour of eyes:* |
| *Hobbies:* | *Favourite groups:* |
| *Sister's name:* | *Sister's age:*                    (9) |

Check your answers with page 28. If you got over 7/10, well done! Try the Stage 2 questions next.

---

*STAGE 2*

Your friend Janice has got her first penfriend letter from Daniela in Berlin. It is quite easy to understand, except for the second paragraph which she wants your help with.

Read the second paragraph carefully. Some words will be easy: *Vielen Dank, Brief, Deutsch, Post, Telefon.* You may need help with some others:

*Tage:* plural of *Tag*
*überrascht* = surprised
*angerufen:* from *anrufen* = to phone
*verstehen* = to understand
*kaputt* = broken
*weil* = because

Check page 28 to see if you have understood.

Read the paragraph again. Now write down what you would say to Janice about that difficult paragraph.

Janice Boyd
77 Onslow Street
Craigshill
Livingston
West Lothian
Scotland

★ ★ Daniela Dunst
★ Leuningerpfad 3
★ 1000 Berlin 13
germany

Liebe Janice,

hier schreibt Daniela aus Berlin. Wie ist das Wetter in Livingston? Heute scheint in Berlin die Sonne. Vielen Dank für Deinen netten Brief. Du kannst gut Deutsch schreiben. Dein Brief ist lange gegangen mit der Post, 19 Tage! Ich war ganz überrascht als du mich angerufen hast. Ich konnte Dich am Telefon nicht sehr gut verstehen, weil das Telefon kaput war.

Mein Steckbrief:
Ich habe braune Haare und braune Augen.

Mein Geburtstag ist am 20th april. Ich werde dieses Jahr 14 Jahre alt. Ich bin 1,75 m groß. Ich habe eine Schwester, sie heißt Kerstin und ist 17 Jahre alt. Sie hat auch braune Haare.

Meine Hobbys sind: Musik, Disco, Schallplatten kaufen. Meine Lieblingsgruppen sind: Discomusik, Supertramp, Alan Sorrenti (Italy), Alan parson project.

Ich gehe jeden Samstag in die Disco. Die Disco heißt "Riverboat".

Ich werde auch in meinen Briefen etwas Deutsch und etwas Englisch schreiben.

Ich mache dann Schluß. Bis zum nächsten Brief.

Herzliche Grüße
Deine
Daniela

for Janice

keep Smiling!

## LETTER 3

*STAGE 1*

Your friend is interested in this letter from your penfriend Norbert, but is not as good at German as you are. Below are some of the questions your friend asks:

**1**   Is Norbert a boy or a girl?                                                    (1)

**2**   The parents are going on holiday. Where to?                          (1)

**3**   Where is Norbert going to stay while they're away?              (1)

**4**   What does Norbert say about the cousin?                             (2)

**5**   What is happening in January?                                             (1)

Norbert asks you four questions in the letter. Write a short letter back to him in English. Be sure to answer all four questions.                                            (4)

---

*STAGE 2*

Your penfriend Norbert has some interesting pieces of news for you in his latest letter about the holidays, a party and his plans for January.

How much did you understand of it all? Check with the answers on page 28. If you got more than 6 points, answer Norbert's letter, writing as much in German as you can.

Hallo Pat!

Ich konnte leider nicht früher schreiben, da ich in letzter Zeit viel zu tun hatte, doch jetzt habe ich Herbstferien.

Wie geht es Dir? Ich hoffe es geht Dir gut. Am Montag fahren meine Eltern in Urlaub, dann bin ich für zwei Wochen ganz alleine zu Hause. Sie fliegen nach Teneriffa.

In der nächsten Woche hat mein Cousin Geburtstag. Dann will er eine große Party halten, auf die auch ich eingeladen bin und noch 15 andere Jungen und Mädchen. Ich freue mich schon sehr darauf und glaube, daß wir viel Spaß bekommen werden. Gehst Du manchmal auch auf große Partys von Freunden? Ich finde das toll. Und Du?

Nächstes Jahr im Januar gehe ich mit ein paar Freunden zur Tanzschule. Warst Du auch schon bei einer Tanzschule?

Ich hoffe, daß Du alles verstehen konntest, was ich geschrieben habe.

Schreib bald wieder

Norbert

## LETTER 4

### STAGE 1

Opposite is a letter from your penfriend Frank, who writes in German. Write back a letter in English, answering any questions and taking up any points he mentions in his letter.
    You might need some help with the following German words and expressions:

*geschrieben* = written
*abgeschickt* = sent
*Ich hoffe, der Brief kommt bei dir heil an* = I hope you got the letter OK
*deswegen* = therefore
*schicken* = send
*wäre* = would be
*jetzt mal was über* = now for something about . . .
*Stunden* = lessons
*jeden* = every
*anfangen* = to begin

    When you have finished, check with the answers on page 29 for some things you might have mentioned in your reply.

(1 mark each out of
total of 7)

### STAGE 2

Opposite is a letter to you from your penfriend Frank.

**1**     What excuse are you going to have ready in answer to Frank's first question?     (1)

**2(a)** Why is Frank writing to you in German?     (1)
  **(b)** What language will you write to him in? Why?     (1)

**3**     What must you not forget to enclose when you write to Frank?     (1)

**4**     How does your school day compare with Frank's?     (2)

Check with the answers on page 29.

Now compose a letter, *as much as possible in German*, to Frank.

### Some suggestions

(a)    Give a good excuse to his first question.
(b)    Answer all his other questions.
(c)    Make some comment about what you have enclosed.
(d)    Tell Frank something about your school timetable.
(e)    Tell him you will write again soon.

Hildesheim

Hallo!

Warum hast Du mir nicht geschrieben? Ich habe einen Brief von mir am 23. Dezember abgeschickt. Ich hoffe der Brief kommt bei Dir heil an. Ich kann nicht so gut Englisch, deswegen schreibe ich in Deutsch.

Kannst Du mir ein Foto von Dir schicken? Ich wäre sehr glücklich. So, jetzt mal was über unsere Schule. Unser Englischlehrer heißt Mr. Hesse. Wir haben Dienstag und Mittwoch sechs Stunden sonst haben wir jeden Tag fünf Stunden. Unsere Schule fängt um 8⁰⁰ Uhr an.

Tschüß
in Liebe
Frank

P.S.: Schreib bitte schnell.

## LETTER 5

*STAGE 1*

Sabine is your new German penfriend. Opposite is her reply to your first letter to her. All you knew about her previously was that she is 12 and that she lives in Wingendorf. Now you should be able to find out more.

**1**   What are her hobbies?                                                                (4)

**2**   When do her holidays end?                                                          (2)

**3**   How many are there in her family?                                            (1)

**4**   She asks a question: can you find out what it means?            (1)

Check your answers with page 29.

Now write a short reply, mainly in English, including an answer to the question that is asked.

---

*STAGE 2*

Sabine is your new German penfriend. Opposite is her first letter to you.

**1**   Do you think she is the right sort of penfriend for you? Why or why not? Think about what she likes doing in her spare time — if she came to stay with you, would you agree about how to spend your time?

**2**   She tells you a little about her house. Would you like to stay in a house like that? Why or why not?

**3**   'Jetzt bist Du wieder mit dem Schreiben dran' — what are *you* going to do now?

**4**   OK — do it!

Wingendorf

Liebe Amanda!

Ich habe mich sehr über Deinen Brief gefreut. In der Schule habe ich schon seit dem 5. Schuljahr Englisch. Ich bin 12 Jahre alt. Meine Hobbys außer Reiten und Popmusik sind: Lesen und vielleicht noch Schwimmen. Unser Haus liegt direkt am Wald. Wir haben ein großes Grundstück mit Wiesen und einen Garten. Bis nächste Woche Donnerstag habe ich noch Herbstferien. Jeden Tag sind meine Eltern und ich zusammen weggefahren. Vorgestern waren wir in einer Reitschule, wo ich geritten bin. Es gibt einfach nichts schöneres, als reiten. Ich habe keine Geschwister, aber dafür genug Freundinen. Lebst du in einer Stadt, oder in einem Dorf? Wir wohnen in einem Dorf. Jetzt bist Du wieder mit dem Schreiben dran.

P.S. Entschuldige bitte,
daß ich so spät ge-
schrieben habe.

P.S. Ich freue mich
auf Deinen nächsten Brief.

Viele Grüße
von Deiner

Brieffreundin

Sabine

## LETTER 6

*STAGE 1*

In the playground you found the letter opposite with no indication as to who it belongs to except the name Peter. In your year group there are several Peters.

Here are some details about them. Which Peter do you think the letter belongs to and why?

*Aufkleber* = sticker
*Button* = badge

(6 marks)

*Peter Taylor* Born in November. Likes football. Has been to Germany. Crazy about pop music. A friend of Alan's.

*Peter Brown* Very good at German. Shy and quiet. Likes tea. Wears school uniform. In Germany on school exchange last year.

*Peter Rankin* Belongs to CND. Keen on girls. Goes around covered in various badges. Has never been to Germany.

*Peter MacDonald* Friend of Alan. Member of CND. Was in Germany on school trip. Has loads of girlfriends.

*Peter MacFeat* Was in Germany on school trip. Knows Alan. Belongs to War Games Club. Very good at German. No time for girls.

---

*STAGE 2*

You are Peter. Opposite is a letter from Nicola Geralski, whom you met when you were in Germany. With your last letter you sent some badges and stickers.

1   What is her reaction to them? (2)

2   Why do you think she mentions 21 November? (1)

3   Does she expect you to write back?
    What makes you think that? (4)

Now reply to Nicola's letter, saying as much as you can in German.

Hallo Peter!

Danke für deinen Brief, die Aufkleber und den Button. Ich habe mich sehr gefreut.
Es wäre toll (fantastic) wenn du mir noch andere Sachen schicken möchtest, ich interessiere mich sehr dafür, wie Du ja weißt! Ich habe auch einen Brief von dem ALAN bekommen.
Ich fand die Ferien so einigermaßen (not so good sometimes!!)
Ich habe am 21. November Geburtstag, Eva kommt dann mit, und auch die Doris und noch zwei andere Mädchen. We drink than tea. You like tea, tea too, very good!
Wenn Du willst, kannst du mir mal wieder schreiben!

    Viel Glück,
        und noch mals
    Danke!
    Dein Nicola
        Geralski

What's the sense of the organisation CND?

# LETTER 7

*STAGE 1*

You have just started writing to a German penfriend and opposite is her answer to your first letter. Your mum is interested to hear what she has to say.

1  Will you be replying to her in English or German? Why?                                    (2)

2  Does Petra already know anything about Scotland? If so, how come?                          (2)

3  What are her hobbies and interests? How do they compare with yours?                        (4)

4  Your mum suggests sending Petra a photo of your house. Is there anything else she might like?                                                                                    (1)

5  Now reply to the letter in English answering Petra's questions.

Check your answers and letter with page 30 when you have finished.

---

*STAGE 2*

Opposite is a letter from your penfriend Petra. Write a letter in reply (does she expect you to write in English or German?) taking up the topics she mentions in her letter and answer her questions. Check with the answers on page 30 once you have written to see that you have covered all the topics she mentions.

She mentions four topics and asks three questions.

Hallo, Jane!

Viele Grüße aus Deutschland sendet Dir Petra.
Ich habe mich sehr über Deinen Brief gefreut.
Er kam heute bei mir an. Die Idee, daß ich in
Deutsch und Du in Englisch schreibst, finde ich
klasse.
Mein Bruder war vor vier Jahren auch in Schottland,
mit der Schule. Deshalb habe ich auch ein paar
Bilder von Schottland. Vielleicht fahre ich nächstes
Jahr mit meiner Klasse nach Schottland.
Fährst Du auch mit Deiner Klasse nach Deutschland?
        Daß Du Dich für Speedway interessierst,
finde ich toll. Ich habe ja ein ähnliches Interesse,
und das ist das Crossfahren und Motorräder.
Mein besonderes Hobby ist die Musik. Besonders gerne
höre ich ELO, Supertramp, Cliff Richard, und
als deutschen Sänger Peter Maffay. Was ist Deine
Lieblingsgruppe?
Jane, würdest Du mir eine große Bitte erfüllen
und mir ein Foto von Dir schicken?
So, nun mache ich langsam Schluß. Den Brief
nehme ich am Montag mit zur Post.

Viele Grüße noch einmal an Deine
Eltern und Deinen Bruder sendet Dir

Deine Brieffreundin    Petra

## LETTER 8

*STAGE 1*

Opposite is your latest letter from your penfriend Iris. The questions below are intended to see if you have got the gist of what she is telling you.

Check your answers with page 30.

**1**  Are you likely to get many letters from Iris, do you think? Why?        (3)

**2**  What does Iris do in her spare time? Do you do the same things?        (3)

**3**  What information will you give when you next write?        (2)

*STAGE 2*

*Do this exercise with a partner.*

Opposite is your latest letter from your penfriend Iris. Your partner wants to know something about Iris. Read the letter together and see how much you can understand. Take notes about what the letter says, and check your notes against the summary in the answers on page 30.

Then answer the letter (in German as much as possible). You can do this with your partner if you like.

(6 marks for understanding topics)

Dear

What have you fore a telephone number? My telefone
number is: 02381 / 25 38 2. Please, give me your
telephone number! Was für eine Gruppe im Singen
hörst Du am liebsten? Ich höre Smokie, Promisis, Status
Quo und die Beatles gerne. Ich habe nichts zu tun,
darum schreibe ich Dir auch so viel. Hast Du
viele Hausaufgaben auf? Ich hatte heute nur
Mathe auf, aber sonst habe ich viel auf.
Ich gehe manchmal raus rodeln (= to boganning),
aber meistens bleibe ich zu Hause und lese oder
gucke Fernsehen. Ich schreibe sehr gerne Briefe!
Ja auch: Wie alt sind Tracy, Nadine, Deine Mutter
und Dein Vater? Mein Bruder wird 7 Jahre alt,
meine Mutter wird 32 Jahre, mein Vater wird 35 Jahre
und ich werde 13 Jahre alt. Hoffentlich verstehst Du
auch das, was ich schreibe. Ich schreibe manches in
Englisch, weil Du es in Deutsch vielleicht nicht
verstehst.
Grüße nochmal alle von uns!

                    Deine Iris

## LETTER 9

*STAGE 1*

You are Peter. Opposite is another letter from Nicola (see letter 6). Check that you have understood the gist of the letter by quickly answering the questions below:

**1** What is Nicola thanking you for? (2)

**2** What was the weather like when Nicola wrote to you? (1)

**3** What age is Nicola now? (1)

**4** In the last paragraph Nicola asks you three questions. What is she asking you? (3)

Now write a short reply to Nicola's letter in English.

---

*STAGE 2*

You are Peter.

Opposite is another letter from your penfriend Nicola (see letter 6). Nicola asks you four questions in her letter. Write back, as much in German as possible, answering Nicola's questions and adding anything else you want to say.

Ask your teacher to mark your letter.

Hallo Peter!

Vielen Dank für dein Poster und die Glückwünsche zu meinem Geburtstag, ich habe mich sehr gefreut.

Ich weiß noch nicht was ich zu Weihnachten mache, nichts besonderes glaube ich. Und was hast Du dir vorgenommen für Weihnachten?

Bei uns schneit es, ich werde gleich erst mal spazieren gehen.

Mein Geburtstag war unheimlich gut, wir haben viel Spaß gehabt. Eva + ich haben Gitarre gespielt, und gesungen. Die Doris, die Nachbarin von Eva war auch da und noch zwei andere.

Ich bin 14 geworden. Du bist schon 14. Wann hast Du Geburtstag? Was wünscht Du dir zu Weihnachten? Ich mir nichts Besonderes. Ich freue mich auf die Weihnachts Ferien. Wann bekommt ihr Ferien? Wir am 23. 11. 81, dieses Jahr sehr spät. Ich werde Dir auch zurückschreiben, wenn Du mir schreibst.

Bis bald, Peter
Tschüß

Deine
Nicola

21

## LETTER 10

*STAGE 1*

*Do this exercise with a partner.*

   Opposite is a long letter to you from your penfriend Norbert. It is quite hard, so here is some help.

   Look at paragraph 1. Norbert is talking about your last letter which was in German. He says, 'Es waren zwar noch einige Fehler darin'.

*einige Fehler* = some mistakes
But he continues, 'ich habe alles verstanden'.

1(a) Was your German perfect? (1)
  (b) Did Norbert manage to understand it? (1)

Now look near the middle of the first page, where he mentions 'Sommerzeugnisse'. These are school reports.
2   What two things happen on 20 June? (2)

Norbert goes on to talk about England (London).
3   Who is in London just now? (1)

4   He says, 'Vielleicht könnten wir uns dann ja mal treffen' — perhaps you could meet up then. When is he talking about? (1)

Tomorrow his neighbours (*Nachbarn*) are expecting a visit from someone.
5   Who is it? Where do they come from? (2)

Check your answers with page 31. More than five out of eight on this letter is a very good mark.

---

*STAGE 2*

You have received this letter from your German penfriend Norbert congratulating you on how well you wrote to him in German last time.
   Check that you understand what he is telling you by answering the following:

1   Have you always written to him in German? (1)

2   In what subject does he have a test tomorrow? (1)

3   How long are Norbert's summer holidays? (1)

4   Two classes from Norbert's school are not at school at the moment.
    Where are they? (1)

5   Where might his class be going next year? (1)

6   Someone is visiting Norbert's neighbours soon.
    Where is this person from? (1)

7   Why does Norbert not have a lot of time to spend on letter-writing tonight? (1)

Check your answers with page 31. If you got more than five out of seven write a letter to Norbert, as much as possible in German, dealing with the points he raises in his letter to you.

Neuss 22

Liebe Margaret!

Vor ein paar Tagen habe ich Deinen Brief bekommen, den Du zum ersten Mal in Deutsch geschrieben hast. Es waren zwar noch einige Fehler darin, aber ich habe alles verstanden.

Es ist ganz interessant zu sehen, welche Schwierigkeiten Ihr Engländer noch mit der deutschen Sprache habt. Aber umgekehrt ist es ja genauso.

Ich habe heute leider nicht soviel Zeit, deshalb schreibe ich in Deutsch.

Morgen schreibe ich eine Arbeit in Deutsch über Lebenslauf und Bewerbung.

Wann bekommt Ihr Eure Sommerferien? Wir bekommen sie am 20. Juni. Das ist der letzte Schultag, dann bekommen wir sechs Wochen Ferien.

Aus unserer Schule sind gerade 2 Klassen in England (London). Sie wohnen in Familien und werden morgens zur U-Bahn gebracht. Vielleicht machen wir im Sommer des nächsten Jahres auch eine Klassenfahrt nach London. Wenn das der Fall ist, dann werde ich Dir das vorher schreiben.

Vielleicht könnten wir uns dann ja mal treffen. Aber wie ich ja sagte, ist das noch lange nicht sicher. Es wäre natürlich toll, wenn wir uns irgendeinmal treffen könnten.

Na ja, und was gibt es bei Dir neues? Was macht bei Dir die Wahlzentik? Ich wünsche Dir, daß Du eine gute Prüfung hattest.

Morgen bekommen unsere Nachbarn Besuch von einem Austauschschüler. Es ist ein Mädchen, das aus Paris kommt.

Nun muß ich Schluß machen, denn ich muß noch ein wenig für die Arbeit üben.

Viele Grüße, und schreibe bald.

Norbert

Abenberg

Liebe Siobhan!

Wie geht es Dir? Mir geht's gut!
Vielen Dank für das Magazin.
Du hast mir mal erzählt, daß Du im Dezember
Geburtstag hast. An welchem Tag?
Ich habe am 18. Dezember. Mein Jahrgang
ist '66.
Gehst Du gern in Kinos? Ich gehe sehr gern.
Ab und zu gehe ich mit meiner Schwester
ins Kino. Ich komme ja nicht oft ins Kino,
da ich in einem Internat bin und nur alle
2 Wochen nach Hause komme.
Meine Ferien dauern 2 Wochen, und zwar
vom 26.5.82 - 6.6.82. In den Ferien bin ich
in Bregenz (mit meinem Vater, Kater, Schwester
und Bruder.). Mein Kater heißt Peter.
So, nun mach' ich Schluß!

Deine Chris

P.S.: Bitte schreib' bald!

Abenberg

Liebe Siobhan!

Vielen Dank für Deinen Brief. Es tut mir leid,
daß ich Dir nicht geschrieben habe aber ich
mußte auf meine letzten Schulaufgaben
sehr viel lernen.
Meine Ferien beginnen am 31. Juli und enden
am 15. September. Ich fahre 2 Wochen zu
meiner Tante nach München.
Nun kann ich Dir auch ein Foto von mir
schicken. Bis jetzt hatte ich immer keins.
        Nun möchte ich Dir noch etwas
über meine Familie schreiben.
Mein Vater ist von Beruf Maschinenbau-
ingenieur, meine Schwester arbeitet als
Steuergehilfin. Mein Bruder studiert und
meine Mutter war Hausfrau. Leider ist
meine Mutter schon tot. Sie ist letztes
Jahr mit 54 Jahren an Lungenkrebs
gestorben.
So, nun mache ich Schluß.

                Tschüß

                Deine Chris

Abenberg

Hallo, Siobhan!

Vielen Dank für Deinen Brief!
Zu Beginn, möchte ich gleich Deine Fragen beantworten.
Ich habe auch ein Haustier. Es ist eine Perserkatze.
Sie heißt Gina. Neulich machten wir ihr einen
Kratzbaum. Sie geht mit Begeisterung daran.
Sie ist noch nicht ganz ein halbes Jahr alt.
Wir haben sie 1½ Monate.
Übrigens; wir tragen keine Schuluniform.
Am Wochenende gehen wir oft spazieren.
Manchmal muß ich auch lernen. Aber das
meiste ist Freizeit. Sonntags gehen wir
um 10 Uhr in die Kirche. Anschließend
essen wir zu Mittag.
Habe ich Dir schon einmal meinen Tagesablauf
geschildert?
Wann hast Du Ferien gehabt? Wo warst Du
in den Ferien?
Ich war zuerst in München und dann in
Tirol ( Tirol ist ein Bundesland in Österreich ).
Danach war ich in Leonberg mit meiner Schwester
und ihrem Freund. Der Freund meiner Schwester
wohnt in Leonberg.
So, nun mach ich Schluß, mir fällt nichts
mehr ein.

Tschüß

Deine Chris

Kirchstr. 27
4100 Duisburg 17
den 11. Dezember

Dear Amanda,

Vielen Dank für Dein liebes Päckchen und den
Brief. Ich habe mich sehr gefreut.
Das Bildchen hat einen schönen Platz in
meinem Setzkasten bekommen.
Ich hoffe Du freust Dich auch ein wenig über
mein Geschenk.
Diesmal schreibe ich dir nochmal in Deutsch,
doch meinen nächsten Brief erhälst Du in
Englisch. Okay? Was wünscht Du Dir denn zu
Weihnachten? Ich bekomme einen neuen Platten-
spieler mit 2 Kassettenrekordern und Radio.
Ich freue mich schon riesig auf den Augen-
blick, wenn ich ihn benutzen darf.
Dein Deutsch ist doch schon sehr gut.
Wielange lernst du schon Deutsch?
Ich hoffe ja, dass ich mal gut Englisch
sprechen kann, so dass wir uns auch mal
sehen können. Wär' das nicht toll?
Welche Pop-Gruppen findest Du denn am
besten? Kennst Du die Gruppe „Nena"?
Es ist meine Lieblingsgruppe.
Wann bekommt ihr eigentlich Weihnachts-
ferien? Unsere beginnen am 23.12. Ich freue
mich schon wahnsinnig, denn in letzter
Zeit schreiben wir unheimlich viele Arbeiten.
So, nun werde ich mal schliessen.
Bitte antworte schnell. O.K.? Danke.
Noch schöne Ferien!

Love and best wishes
Sabine

P.S.: auch viele Grüsse and
best wishes to your family!

# ANSWERS

*Letter 1, Stage 1*

1  Girl.
2  Anja Angerstein.
3  12.
4  Fair hair; blue eyes.

5  Dancing, pop music, English, cycling
   (any 3 = 3 marks).
6  Abba, Smokie, John Travolta
   (any 2 = 2 marks).

*Letter 1, Stage 2*

In your reply you should mention:

What you look like;
Your hobbies;
What singers you like;
What class you are in.

   Ask your teacher to help you correct any serious mistakes in your German.

---

*Letter 2, Stage 1*

1  Sunny.
2  *Name:* Daniela Dunst
   *Birthday:* 20 April
   *Colour of eyes:* brown
   *Hobbies:* music, discos, records
   *Sister's name:* Kerstin

   *Age:* 14 this year
   *Height:* 1.75m
   *Favourite groups:* Discomusik, Supertramp,
   Alan Sorrenti, Alan Parson Project
   *Sister's age:* 17

*Letter 2, Stage 2*

She says: 'Thank you for your letter. You write German well. Your letter took a long time to arrive —
19 days. I was really surprised when you phoned me. I couldn't understand you very well on the phone,
because the phone was broken'.

---

*Letter 3, Stage 1*

1  A boy.
2  Tenerife.
3  At home on his own.

4  It is his birthday; there will be a party.
5  He is going to dancing classes.

In your reply you should have given the following information:

how you are; whether you sometimes go to friends' parties, whether you think they're great as well;
whether you have ever been to dancing classes.

*Letter 3, Stage 2*

He is staying at home alone; his parents are off to Tenerife on Monday; for two weeks.
It is his cousin's birthday next week; he is having a big party to which Norbert is invited; fifteen other boys
and girls are going; he thinks it will be great.
He is going to dancing classes with some friends.

(8 points)

*Letter 4, Stage 1*

You might have mentioned (1 mark each):

Why you have not written;
If you got his letter of 23 December;
If you are sending him a photo;
Something about how your school compares with his;
Your German teacher's name;
The length of the school day;
What time it starts.

*Letter 4, Stage 2*

1    Any excuse as to why you have not written.
2(a) His English is not so good.
  (b) Any good reason.
3    A photo.
4    You must mention when school begins and how many periods you have.

---

*Letter 5, Stage 1*

1    Riding, pop music, reading, swimming.
2    Thursday, next week.
3    Just herself and her parents — 'Ich habe keine Geschwister'.
4    The question is: Do you live in a town or village?

*Letter 5, Stage 2*

Ask your teacher to check your answers to this one.

---

*Letter 6, Stage 1*

The letter belongs to Peter MacDonald. This is because:

Peter has sent Nicola badges and stickers.
He knows Alan.
He must know who Eva and Doris are, and since Nicola is also a girl, it's likely he is keen on girls.
He must have been in Germany to get to know them.
He must have mentioned CND in a letter so he is likely to be a member.

*Letter 6, Stage 2*

1    She's very pleased. She'd like you to send more things.
2    It's her birthday.
3    Yes. She asks you for more badges and an explanation of what CND is, so she's obviously expecting a
     letter. She also says, 'You can write to me again if you like.'

*Letter 7, Stage 1*

1   English. You agreed that she would write in German, you in English.
2   Yes, her brother was over here.
3   Motorcross, motorbikes and music. You, Jane, must have said you were keen on Speedway, so you have that in common.
4   A photo of you.
5   Answer the questions:
    Are you also going with your class to Germany?
    What is your favourite group?
    Can you send me a photo of yourself?

*Letter 7, Stage 2*

Topics:

Your last letter,
Scotland,
Motorsports: Speedway and Motorcross.
Music:  ELO, Supertramp and Cliff Richard.
Questions:  Are you coming to Germany with your class? What is your favourite group? Can you send a photo of yourself?

---

*Letter 8, Stage 1*

1   Yes. She hasn't much to do — 'Ich habe nichts zu tun'.
    She likes writing letters — 'Ich schreibe sehr gerne Briefe'.
2   Iris likes: Smokie, Status Quo, The Beatles and Promises; tobogganing; watching TV; writing letters (any 3 hobbies you mention — 3 marks).
3   You'll tell her if you have a lot of homework; the ages of the people she mentions — Tracy, Nadine, your parents.

*Letter 8, Stage 2*

Summary:  (1 mark per topic)

What group do you like best? She names her favourites.
She writes a lot of letters because she has nothing to do.
Have you lots of homework? She has.
She likes tobogganing, staying at home watching TV and reading.
She likes writing letters. She wants to know people's ages and tells you about her family.
She hopes you understand what she writes.

---

*Letter 9, Stage 1*

1   A poster and your birthday wishes.
2   It was snowing.
3   14.
4   When is your birthday? What do you want for Christmas? When are your holidays?

*Letter 9, Stage 2*

Ask your teacher to mark this letter.

*Letter 10, Stage 1*

**1(a)** No.  **(b)** Yes.
**2**   They got their school reports and it was the end of term.
**3**   Two classes from Norbert's school.
**4**   Next summer. (He may be coming to London with his class.)
**5**   A girl from Paris.

*Letter 10, Stage 2*

**1**   No. (Your last letter was the first you had written in German.)
**2**   German.
**3**   Six weeks.
**4**   London.
**5**   London.
**6**   Paris.
**7**   He has to study for his test.

# RECORD OF WORK

Name: ................................................................Class: ................................

When you have completed the tasks in the letters, copy out and fill in the form below, with
a tick for each completed letter, the date and your mark (if appropriate). Please also put a
tick in the appropriate column if you replied to the letter. Give your completed work to
your teacher and ask him/her to put his/her initials in the column marked 'Teacher'.

|  | Completed | Date | Mark | Replied in English | Replied in English & German | Replied in German | Teacher |
|---|---|---|---|---|---|---|---|
| Letter 1, Stage 1 |  |  |  |  |  |  |  |
| Letter 1, Stage 2 |  |  |  |  |  |  |  |
| Letter 2, Stage 1 |  |  |  |  |  |  |  |
| Letter 2, Stage 2 |  |  |  |  |  |  |  |
| Letter 3, Stage 1 |  |  |  |  |  |  |  |
| Letter 3, Stage 2 |  |  |  |  |  |  |  |
| Letter 4, Stage 1 |  |  |  |  |  |  |  |
| Letter 4, Stage 2 |  |  |  |  |  |  |  |
| Letter 5, Stage 1 |  |  |  |  |  |  |  |
| Letter 5, Stage 2 |  |  |  |  |  |  |  |
| Letter 6, Stage 1 |  |  |  |  |  |  |  |
| Letter 6, Stage 2 |  |  |  |  |  |  |  |
| Letter 7, Stage 1 |  |  |  |  |  |  |  |
| Letter 7, Stage 2 |  |  |  |  |  |  |  |
| Letter 8, Stage 1 |  |  |  |  |  |  |  |
| Letter 8, Stage 2 |  |  |  |  |  |  |  |
| Letter 9, Stage 1 |  |  |  |  |  |  |  |
| Letter 9, Stage 2 |  |  |  |  |  |  |  |
| Letter 10, Stage 1 |  |  |  |  |  |  |  |
| Letter 10, Stage 2 |  |  |  |  |  |  |  |